Personal Firearms Record Book

Property Of: _____

<u>A Complete Record Log for up to 75 Firearms</u>

::Second Amendment::

<u>The Original Homeland Security:</u>

A well regulated Militia, being necessary to the security of a free State, the right of the people to keep and bear Arms, shall not be infringed!!!

Copyright © 2012 Brian S. Bowers

All rights reserved.

Personal Firearms Record Book

Copyright © 2012 Brian S. Bowers

All rights reserved.

ISBN-10: 1481829750
ISBN-13: 978-1481829755

DEDICATION

Dedicated to Freedom. American Gun Owners support our freedoms by keeping tyranny in check. Without private Gun Ownership, no other rights would be safe..

ACKNOWLEDGMENTS

As with all Law Abiding Gun Owners and dedicated Patriots of this great Nation. I would like to place all acknowledgements to the Founding Fathers. They saw the need to protect the freedoms they described with one, very powerful right/freedom. The right to keep and bear Arms..

Personal Firearms Basic Ownership Datasheet

Firearm Type:	rifle - handgun - shotgun - airgun - black powder other:	Serial Number:	
Manufacturer:		Other Id No.:	
Caliber:		Capacity:	
Model/Type:		Weight:	
Barrel Length		Barrel Type:	Standard - Target - Bull - Other:
Finish:	Blue - Stainless - Parkerized - Plated (type): _____ other: _____		
Action: Circle all that apply	revolver - single shot - semiauto - full auto - lever - bolt - pump - top break - over/under - side by side - single action - double action - double action auto - muzzle loader		
Sight Type:		Stock Type:	
Scope Info:		Rings/Bases:	

Acquisition Information

Obtained From:		Id No.:	
Name and address		DOB:	
		Relationship:	
		Date Purchased:	
Price Paid:	$	Replacement Value:	$

Special Or Specific Information

Accessories:		Best Load:	
Special Marks Or Cartouches:		Maint Info:	
Other Notes:			

Disposition Information

If I should die I want this firearm to go to:			
Gun Sold To:		Id No.:	
Name and address		DOB:	
		Relationship:	
		Date Sold:	
Selling Price:	$	Lost/Stolen:	

Additional Notes:

Photo:

Personal Firearms Basic Ownership Datasheet

Firearm Type:	rifle - handgun - shotgun - airgun - black powder other:	**Serial Number:**	
Manufacturer:		**Other Id No.:**	
Caliber:		**Capacity:**	
Model/Type:		**Weight:**	
Barrel Length		**Barrel Type:**	Standard - Target - Bull - Other:
Finish:	Blue - Stainless - Parkerized - Plated (type): _____ other: _____		
Action: Circle all that apply	revolver - single shot - semiauto - full auto - lever - bolt - pump - top break - over/under - side by side - single action - double action - double action auto - muzzle loader		
Sight Type:		**Stock Type:**	
Scope Info:		**Rings/Bases:**	

Acquisition Information

Obtained From:		**Id No.:**	
Name and address		**DOB:**	
		Relationship:	
		Date Purchased:	
Price Paid:	$	**Replacement Value:**	$

Special Or Specific Information

Accessories:		**Best Load:**	
Special Marks Or Cartouches:		**Maint Info:**	
Other Notes:			

Disposition Information

If I should die I want this firearm to go to:			
Gun Sold To:		**Id No.:**	
Name and address		**DOB:**	
		Relationship:	
		Date Sold:	
Selling Price:	$	**Lost/Stolen:**	

Additional Notes:

Photo:

Personal Firearms Basic Ownership Datasheet

Firearm Type:	rifle - handgun - shotgun - airgun - black powder other:	**Serial Number:**	
Manufacturer:		**Other Id No.:**	
Caliber:		**Capacity:**	
Model/Type:		**Weight:**	
Barrel Length		**Barrel Type:**	Standard - Target - Bull - Other:
Finish:	Blue - Stainless - Parkerized - Plated (type): _____ other: _____		
Action: Circle all that apply	revolver - single shot - semiauto - full auto - lever - bolt - pump - top break - over/under - side by side - single action - double action - double action auto - muzzle loader		
Sight Type:		**Stock Type:**	
Scope Info:		**Rings/Bases:**	

Acquisition Information

Obtained From:		**Id No.:**	
Name and address		**DOB:**	
		Relationship:	
		Date Purchased:	
Price Paid:	$	**Replacement Value:**	$

Special Or Specific Information

Accessories:		**Best Load:**	
Special Marks Or Cartouches:		**Maint Info:**	
Other Notes:			

Disposition Information

If I should die I want this firearm to go to:			
Gun Sold To:		**Id No.:**	
Name and address		**DOB:**	
		Relationship:	
		Date Sold:	
Selling Price:	$	**Lost/Stolen:**	

Additional Notes:

Photo:

Personal Firearms Basic Ownership Datasheet

Firearm Type:	rifle - handgun - shotgun - airgun - black powder other:	**Serial Number:**	
Manufacturer:		**Other Id No.:**	
Caliber:		**Capacity:**	
Model/Type:		**Weight:**	
Barrel Length		**Barrel Type:**	Standard - Target - Bull - Other:
Finish:	Blue - Stainless - Parkerized - Plated (type): _____ other: _____		
Action: Circle all that apply	revolver - single shot - semiauto - full auto - lever - bolt - pump - top break - over/under - side by side - single action - double action - double action auto - muzzle loader		
Sight Type:		**Stock Type:**	
Scope Info:		**Rings/Bases:**	

Acquisition Information

Obtained From:		**Id No.:**	
Name and address		**DOB:**	
		Relationship:	
		Date Purchased:	
Price Paid:	$	**Replacement Value:**	$

Special Or Specific Information

Accessories:		**Best Load:**	
Special Marks Or Cartouches:		**Maint Info:**	
Other Notes:			

Disposition Information

If I should die I want this firearm to go to:			
Gun Sold To:		**Id No.:**	
Name and address		**DOB:**	
		Relationship:	
		Date Sold:	
Selling Price:	$	**Lost/Stolen:**	

Additional Notes:

Photo:

Personal Firearms Basic Ownership Datasheet

Firearm Type:	rifle - handgun - shotgun - airgun - black powder other:	Serial Number:	
Manufacturer:		Other Id No.:	
Caliber:		Capacity:	
Model/Type:		Weight:	
Barrel Length		Barrel Type:	Standard - Target - Bull - Other:
Finish:	Blue - Stainless - Parkerized - Plated (type): _____ other: _____		
Action: Circle all that apply	revolver - single shot - semiauto - full auto - lever - bolt - pump - top break - over/under - side by side - single action - double action - double action auto - muzzle loader		
Sight Type:		Stock Type:	
Scope Info:		Rings/Bases:	

Acquisition Information

Obtained From:		Id No.:	
Name and address		DOB:	
		Relationship:	
		Date Purchased:	
Price Paid:	$	Replacement Value:	$

Special Or Specific Information

Accessories:		Best Load:	
Special Marks Or Cartouches:		Maint Info:	
Other Notes:			

Disposition Information

If I should die I want this firearm to go to:			
Gun Sold To:		Id No.:	
Name and address		DOB:	
		Relationship:	
		Date Sold:	
Selling Price:	$	Lost/Stolen:	

Additional Notes:

Photo:

Personal Firearms Basic Ownership Datasheet

Firearm Type:	rifle - handgun - shotgun - airgun - black powder other:	**Serial Number:**	
Manufacturer:		**Other Id No.:**	
Caliber:		**Capacity:**	
Model/Type:		**Weight:**	
Barrel Length		**Barrel Type:**	Standard - Target - Bull - Other:
Finish:	Blue - Stainless - Parkerized - Plated (type): _____ other: _____		
Action: Circle all that apply	revolver - single shot - semiauto - full auto - lever - bolt - pump - top break - over/under - side by side - single action - double action - double action auto - muzzle loader		
Sight Type:		**Stock Type:**	
Scope Info:		**Rings/Bases:**	

Acquisition Information

Obtained From:		**Id No.:**	
Name and address		**DOB:**	
		Relationship:	
		Date Purchased:	
Price Paid:	$	**Replacement Value:**	$

Special Or Specific Information

Accessories:		**Best Load:**	
Special Marks Or Cartouches:		**Maint Info:**	
Other Notes:			

Disposition Information

If I should die I want this firearm to go to:			
Gun Sold To:		**Id No.:**	
Name and address		**DOB:**	
		Relationship:	
		Date Sold:	
Selling Price:	$	**Lost/Stolen:**	

Additional Notes:

Photo:

Personal Firearms Basic Ownership Datasheet

Firearm Type:	rifle - handgun - shotgun - airgun - black powder other:	Serial Number:	
Manufacturer:		Other Id No.:	
Caliber:		Capacity:	
Model/Type:		Weight:	
Barrel Length		Barrel Type:	Standard - Target - Bull - Other:
Finish:	Blue - Stainless - Parkerized - Plated (type): _____ other: _____		
Action: Circle all that apply	revolver - single shot - semiauto - full auto - lever - bolt - pump - top break - over/under - side by side - single action - double action - double action auto - muzzle loader		
Sight Type:		Stock Type:	
Scope Info:		Rings/Bases:	

Acquisition Information

Obtained From:		Id No.:	
Name and address		DOB:	
		Relationship:	
		Date Purchased:	
Price Paid:	$	Replacement Value:	$

Special Or Specific Information

Accessories:		Best Load:	
Special Marks Or Cartouches:		Maint Info:	
Other Notes:			

Disposition Information

If I should die I want this firearm to go to:			
Gun Sold To:		Id No.:	
Name and address		DOB:	
		Relationship:	
		Date Sold:	
Selling Price:	$	Lost/Stolen:	

Additional Notes:

Photo:

Personal Firearms Basic Ownership Datasheet

Firearm Type:	rifle - handgun - shotgun - airgun - black powder other:	**Serial Number:**	
Manufacturer:		**Other Id No.:**	
Caliber:		**Capacity:**	
Model/Type:		**Weight:**	
Barrel Length		**Barrel Type:**	Standard - Target - Bull - Other:
Finish:	Blue - Stainless - Parkerized - Plated (type): _____ other: _____		
Action: Circle all that apply	revolver - single shot - semiauto - full auto - lever - bolt - pump - top break - over/under - side by side - single action - double action - double action auto - muzzle loader		
Sight Type:		**Stock Type:**	
Scope Info:		**Rings/Bases:**	

Acquisition Information

Obtained From:		**Id No.:**	
Name and address		**DOB:**	
		Relationship:	
		Date Purchased:	
Price Paid:	$	**Replacement Value:**	$

Special Or Specific Information

Accessories:		**Best Load:**	
Special Marks Or Cartouches:		**Maint Info:**	
Other Notes:			

Disposition Information

If I should die I want this firearm to go to:			
Gun Sold To:		**Id No.:**	
Name and address		**DOB:**	
		Relationship:	
		Date Sold:	
Selling Price:	$	**Lost/Stolen:**	

Additional Notes:

Photo:

Personal Firearms Basic Ownership Datasheet

Firearm Type:	rifle - handgun - shotgun - airgun - black powder other:	Serial Number:	
Manufacturer:		Other Id No.:	
Caliber:		Capacity:	
Model/Type:		Weight:	
Barrel Length		Barrel Type:	Standard - Target - Bull - Other:
Finish:	Blue - Stainless - Parkerized - Plated (type): _____ other: _____		
Action: Circle all that apply	revolver - single shot - semiauto - full auto - lever - bolt - pump - top break - over/under - side by side - single action - double action - double action auto - muzzle loader		
Sight Type:		Stock Type:	
Scope Info:		Rings/Bases:	

Acquisition Information

Obtained From:		Id No.:	
Name and address		DOB:	
		Relationship:	
		Date Purchased:	
Price Paid:	$	Replacement Value:	$

Special Or Specific Information

Accessories:		Best Load:	
Special Marks Or Cartouches:		Maint Info:	
Other Notes:			

Disposition Information

If I should die I want this firearm to go to:			
Gun Sold To:		Id No.:	
Name and address		DOB:	
		Relationship:	
		Date Sold:	
Selling Price:	$	Lost/Stolen:	

Additional Notes:

Photo:

Personal Firearms Basic Ownership Datasheet				
Firearm Type:	rifle - handgun - shotgun - airgun - black powder other:		Serial Number:	
Manufacturer:			Other Id No.:	
Caliber:			Capacity:	
Model/Type:			Weight:	
Barrel Length			Barrel Type:	Standard - Target - Bull - Other:
Finish:	Blue - Stainless - Parkerized - Plated (type): _____ other: _____			
Action: Circle all that apply	revolver - single shot - semiauto - full auto - lever - bolt - pump - top break - over/under - side by side - single action - double action - double action auto - muzzle loader			
Sight Type:			Stock Type:	
Scope Info:			Rings/Bases:	
Acquisition Information				
Obtained From:			Id No.:	
Name and address			DOB:	
^	^	Relationship:	
^	^	Date Purchased:	
Price Paid:	$		Replacement Value:	$
Special Or Specific Information				
Accessories:			Best Load:	
Special Marks Or Cartouches:			Maint Info:	
Other Notes:				
Disposition Information				
If I should die I want this firearm to go to:			
Gun Sold To:			Id No.:	
Name and address			DOB:	
^	^	Relationship:	
^	^	Date Sold:	
Selling Price:	$		Lost/Stolen:	

Additional Notes:

Photo:

Personal Firearms Basic Ownership Datasheet

Firearm Type:	rifle - handgun - shotgun - airgun - black powder other:	**Serial Number:**	
Manufacturer:		**Other Id No.:**	
Caliber:		**Capacity:**	
Model/Type:		**Weight:**	
Barrel Length		**Barrel Type:**	Standard - Target - Bull - Other:
Finish:	Blue - Stainless - Parkerized - Plated (type): _____ other: _____		
Action: Circle all that apply	revolver - single shot - semiauto - full auto - lever - bolt - pump - top break - over/under - side by side - single action - double action - double action auto - muzzle loader		
Sight Type:		**Stock Type:**	
Scope Info:		**Rings/Bases:**	

Acquisition Information

Obtained From:		**Id No.:**	
		DOB:	
Name and address		**Relationship:**	
		Date Purchased:	
Price Paid:	$	**Replacement Value:**	$

Special Or Specific Information

Accessories:		**Best Load:**	
Special Marks Or Cartouches:		**Maint Info:**	
Other Notes:			

Disposition Information

If I should die I want this firearm to go to:			
Gun Sold To:		**Id No.:**	
		DOB:	
Name and address		**Relationship:**	
		Date Sold:	
Selling Price:	$	**Lost/Stolen:**	

Additional Notes:

Photo:

Personal Firearms Basic Ownership Datasheet

Firearm Type:	rifle - handgun - shotgun - airgun - black powder other:	Serial Number:	
Manufacturer:		Other Id No.:	
Caliber:		Capacity:	
Model/Type:		Weight:	
Barrel Length		Barrel Type:	Standard - Target - Bull - Other:
Finish:	Blue - Stainless - Parkerized - Plated (type): _____ other: _____		
Action: Circle all that apply	revolver - single shot - semiauto - full auto - lever - bolt - pump - top break - over/under - side by side - single action - double action - double action auto - muzzle loader		
Sight Type:		Stock Type:	
Scope Info:		Rings/Bases:	

Acquisition Information

Obtained From:		Id No.:	
Name and address		DOB:	
		Relationship:	
		Date Purchased:	
Price Paid:	$	Replacement Value:	$

Special Or Specific Information

Accessories:		Best Load:	
Special Marks Or Cartouches:		Maint Info:	
Other Notes:			

Disposition Information

If I should die I want this firearm to go to:			
Gun Sold To:		Id No.:	
Name and address		DOB:	
		Relationship:	
		Date Sold:	
Selling Price:	$	Lost/Stolen:	

Additional Notes:

Photo:

Personal Firearms Basic Ownership Datasheet

Firearm Type:	rifle - handgun - shotgun - airgun - black powder other:	**Serial Number:**	
Manufacturer:		**Other Id No.:**	
Caliber:		**Capacity:**	
Model/Type:		**Weight:**	
Barrel Length		**Barrel Type:**	Standard - Target - Bull - Other:
Finish:	Blue - Stainless - Parkerized - Plated (type): _____ other: _____		
Action: Circle all that apply	revolver - single shot - semiauto - full auto - lever - bolt - pump - top break - over/under - side by side - single action - double action - double action auto - muzzle loader		
Sight Type:		**Stock Type:**	
Scope Info:		**Rings/Bases:**	

Acquisition Information

Obtained From:		**Id No.:**	
Name and address		**DOB:**	
		Relationship:	
		Date Purchased:	
Price Paid:	$	**Replacement Value:**	$

Special Or Specific Information

Accessories:		**Best Load:**	
Special Marks Or Cartouches:		**Maint Info:**	
Other Notes:			

Disposition Information

If I should die I want this firearm to go to:

Gun Sold To:		**Id No.:**	
Name and address		**DOB:**	
		Relationship:	
		Date Sold:	
Selling Price:	$	**Lost/Stolen:**	

Additional Notes:

Photo:

Personal Firearms Basic Ownership Datasheet

Firearm Type:	rifle - handgun - shotgun - airgun - black powder other:	**Serial Number:**	
Manufacturer:		**Other Id No.:**	
Caliber:		**Capacity:**	
Model/Type:		**Weight:**	
Barrel Length		**Barrel Type:**	Standard - Target - Bull - Other:
Finish:	Blue - Stainless - Parkerized - Plated (type): _____ other: _____		
Action: Circle all that apply	revolver - single shot - semiauto - full auto - lever - bolt - pump - top break - over/under - side by side - single action - double action - double action auto - muzzle loader		
Sight Type:		**Stock Type:**	
Scope Info:		**Rings/Bases:**	

Acquisition Information

Obtained From:		**Id No.:**	
Name and address		**DOB:**	
		Relationship:	
		Date Purchased:	
Price Paid:	$	**Replacement Value:**	$

Special Or Specific Information

Accessories:		**Best Load:**	
Special Marks Or Cartouches:		**Maint Info:**	
Other Notes:			

Disposition Information

If I should die I want this firearm to go to:			
Gun Sold To:		**Id No.:**	
Name and address		**DOB:**	
		Relationship:	
		Date Sold:	
Selling Price:	$	**Lost/Stolen:**	

Additional Notes:

Photo:

Personal Firearms Basic Ownership Datasheet

Firearm Type:	rifle - handgun - shotgun - airgun - black powder other:	**Serial Number:**	
Manufacturer:		**Other Id No.:**	
Caliber:		**Capacity:**	
Model/Type:		**Weight:**	
Barrel Length		**Barrel Type:**	Standard - Target - Bull - Other:
Finish:	Blue - Stainless - Parkerized - Plated (type): _____ other: _____		
Action: Circle all that apply	revolver - single shot - semiauto - full auto - lever - bolt - pump - top break - over/under - side by side - single action - double action - double action auto - muzzle loader		
Sight Type:		**Stock Type:**	
Scope Info:		**Rings/Bases:**	

Acquisition Information

Obtained From:		**Id No.:**	
		DOB:	
Name and address		**Relationship:**	
		Date Purchased:	
Price Paid:	$	**Replacement Value:**	$

Special Or Specific Information

Accessories:		**Best Load:**	
Special Marks Or Cartouches:		**Maint Info:**	
Other Notes:			

Disposition Information

If I should die I want this firearm to go to:			
Gun Sold To:		**Id No.:**	
		DOB:	
Name and address		**Relationship:**	
		Date Sold:	
Selling Price:	$	**Lost/Stolen:**	

Additional Notes:

Photo:

Personal Firearms Basic Ownership Datasheet

Firearm Type:	rifle - handgun - shotgun - airgun - black powder other:	**Serial Number:**	
Manufacturer:		**Other Id No.:**	
Caliber:		**Capacity:**	
Model/Type:		**Weight:**	
Barrel Length		**Barrel Type:**	Standard - Target - Bull - Other:
Finish:	Blue - Stainless - Parkerized - Plated (type): _____ other: _____		
Action: Circle all that apply	revolver - single shot - semiauto - full auto - lever - bolt - pump - top break - over/under - side by side - single action - double action - double action auto - muzzle loader		
Sight Type:		**Stock Type:**	
Scope Info:		**Rings/Bases:**	

Acquisition Information

Obtained From:		**Id No.:**	
Name and address		**DOB:**	
		Relationship:	
		Date Purchased:	
Price Paid:	$	**Replacement Value:**	$

Special Or Specific Information

Accessories:		**Best Load:**	
Special Marks Or Cartouches:		**Maint Info:**	
Other Notes:			

Disposition Information

If I should die I want this firearm to go to:

Gun Sold To:		**Id No.:**	
Name and address		**DOB:**	
		Relationship:	
		Date Sold:	
Selling Price:	$	**Lost/Stolen:**	

Additional Notes:

Photo:

Personal Firearms Basic Ownership Datasheet

Firearm Type:	rifle - handgun - shotgun - airgun - black powder other:	**Serial Number:**	
Manufacturer:		**Other Id No.:**	
Caliber:		**Capacity:**	
Model/Type:		**Weight:**	
Barrel Length		**Barrel Type:**	Standard - Target - Bull - Other:
Finish:	Blue - Stainless - Parkerized - Plated (type): _____ other: _____		
Action: Circle all that apply	revolver - single shot - semiauto - full auto - lever - bolt - pump - top break - over/under - side by side - single action - double action - double action auto - muzzle loader		
Sight Type:		**Stock Type:**	
Scope Info:		**Rings/Bases:**	

Acquisition Information

Obtained From:		**Id No.:**	
Name and address		**DOB:**	
		Relationship:	
		Date Purchased:	
Price Paid:	$	**Replacement Value:**	$

Special Or Specific Information

Accessories:		**Best Load:**	
Special Marks Or Cartouches:		**Maint Info:**	
Other Notes:			

Disposition Information

If I should die I want this firearm to go to:			
Gun Sold To:		**Id No.:**	
Name and address		**DOB:**	
		Relationship:	
		Date Sold:	
Selling Price:	$	**Lost/Stolen:**	

Additional Notes:

Photo:

Personal Firearms Basic Ownership Datasheet

Firearm Type:	rifle - handgun - shotgun - airgun - black powder other:	Serial Number:	
Manufacturer:		Other Id No.:	
Caliber:		Capacity:	
Model/Type:		Weight:	
Barrel Length		Barrel Type:	Standard - Target - Bull - Other:
Finish:	Blue - Stainless - Parkerized - Plated (type): _____ other: _____		
Action: Circle all that apply	revolver - single shot - semiauto - full auto - lever - bolt - pump - top break - over/under - side by side - single action - double action - double action auto - muzzle loader		
Sight Type:		Stock Type:	
Scope Info:		Rings/Bases:	

Acquisition Information

Obtained From:		Id No.:	
Name and address		DOB:	
		Relationship:	
		Date Purchased:	
Price Paid:	$	Replacement Value:	$

Special Or Specific Information

Accessories:		Best Load:	
Special Marks Or Cartouches:		Maint Info:	
Other Notes:			

Disposition Information

If I should die I want this firearm to go to:			
Gun Sold To:		Id No.:	
Name and address		DOB:	
		Relationship:	
		Date Sold:	
Selling Price:	$	Lost/Stolen:	

Additional Notes:

Photo:

Personal Firearms Basic Ownership Datasheet

Firearm Type:	rifle - handgun - shotgun - airgun - black powder other:	Serial Number:	
Manufacturer:		Other Id No.:	
Caliber:		Capacity:	
Model/Type:		Weight:	
Barrel Length		Barrel Type:	Standard - Target - Bull - Other:
Finish:	Blue - Stainless - Parkerized - Plated (type): _____ other: _____		
Action: Circle all that apply	revolver - single shot - semiauto - full auto - lever - bolt - pump - top break - over/under - side by side - single action - double action - double action auto - muzzle loader		
Sight Type:		Stock Type:	
Scope Info:		Rings/Bases:	

Acquisition Information

Obtained From:		Id No.:	
Name and address		DOB:	
		Relationship:	
		Date Purchased:	
Price Paid:	$	Replacement Value:	$

Special Or Specific Information

Accessories:		Best Load:	
Special Marks Or Cartouches:		Maint Info:	
Other Notes:			

Disposition Information

If I should die I want this firearm to go to:			
Gun Sold To:		Id No.:	
Name and address		DOB:	
		Relationship:	
		Date Sold:	
Selling Price:	$	Lost/Stolen:	

Additional Notes:

Photo:

Personal Firearms Basic Ownership Datasheet

Firearm Type:	rifle - handgun - shotgun - airgun - black powder other:	**Serial Number:**	
Manufacturer:		**Other Id No.:**	
Caliber:		**Capacity:**	
Model/Type:		**Weight:**	
Barrel Length		**Barrel Type:**	Standard - Target - Bull - Other:
Finish:	Blue - Stainless - Parkerized - Plated (type): _____ other: _____		
Action: Circle all that apply	revolver - single shot - semiauto - full auto - lever - bolt - pump - top break - over/under - side by side - single action - double action - double action auto - muzzle loader		
Sight Type:		**Stock Type:**	
Scope Info:		**Rings/Bases:**	

Acquisition Information

Obtained From:		**Id No.:**	
Name and address		**DOB:**	
		Relationship:	
		Date Purchased:	
Price Paid:	$	**Replacement Value:**	$

Special Or Specific Information

Accessories:		**Best Load:**	
Special Marks Or Cartouches:		**Maint Info:**	
Other Notes:			

Disposition Information

If I should die I want this firearm to go to:

Gun Sold To:		**Id No.:**	
Name and address		**DOB:**	
		Relationship:	
		Date Sold:	
Selling Price:	$	**Lost/Stolen:**	

Additional Notes:

Photo:

Personal Firearms Basic Ownership Datasheet

Firearm Type:	rifle - handgun - shotgun - airgun - black powder other:	**Serial Number:**	
Manufacturer:		**Other Id No.:**	
Caliber:		**Capacity:**	
Model/Type:		**Weight:**	
Barrel Length		**Barrel Type:**	Standard - Target - Bull - Other:
Finish:	Blue - Stainless - Parkerized - Plated (type): _____ other: _____		
Action: Circle all that apply	revolver - single shot - semiauto - full auto - lever - bolt - pump - top break - over/under - side by side - single action - double action - double action auto - muzzle loader		
Sight Type:		**Stock Type:**	
Scope Info:		**Rings/Bases:**	

Acquisition Information

Obtained From:		**Id No.:**	
Name and address		**DOB:**	
		Relationship:	
		Date Purchased:	
Price Paid:	$	**Replacement Value:**	$

Special Or Specific Information

Accessories:		**Best Load:**	
Special Marks Or Cartouches:		**Maint Info:**	
Other Notes:			

Disposition Information

If I should die I want this firearm to go to:			
Gun Sold To:		**Id No.:**	
Name and address		**DOB:**	
		Relationship:	
		Date Sold:	
Selling Price:	$	**Lost/Stolen:**	

Additional Notes:

Photo:

Personal Firearms Basic Ownership Datasheet

Firearm Type:	rifle - handgun - shotgun - airgun - black powder other:	**Serial Number:**	
Manufacturer:		**Other Id No.:**	
Caliber:		**Capacity:**	
Model/Type:		**Weight:**	
Barrel Length		**Barrel Type:**	Standard - Target - Bull - Other:
Finish:	Blue - Stainless - Parkerized - Plated (type): _____ other: _____		
Action: Circle all that apply	revolver - single shot - semiauto - full auto - lever - bolt - pump - top break - over/under - side by side - single action - double action - double action auto - muzzle loader		
Sight Type:		**Stock Type:**	
Scope Info:		**Rings/Bases:**	

Acquisition Information

Obtained From:		**Id No.:**	
Name and address		**DOB:**	
		Relationship:	
		Date Purchased:	
Price Paid:	$	**Replacement Value:**	$

Special Or Specific Information

Accessories:		**Best Load:**	
Special Marks Or Cartouches:		**Maint Info:**	
Other Notes:			

Disposition Information

If I should die I want this firearm to go to:			
Gun Sold To:		**Id No.:**	
Name and address		**DOB:**	
		Relationship:	
		Date Sold:	
Selling Price:	$	**Lost/Stolen:**	

Additional Notes:

Photo:

Personal Firearms Basic Ownership Datasheet

Firearm Type:	rifle - handgun - shotgun - airgun - black powder other:	**Serial Number:**	
Manufacturer:		**Other Id No.:**	
Caliber:		**Capacity:**	
Model/Type:		**Weight:**	
Barrel Length		**Barrel Type:**	Standard - Target - Bull - Other:
Finish:	Blue - Stainless - Parkerized - Plated (type): _____ other: _____		
Action: Circle all that apply	revolver - single shot - semiauto - full auto - lever - bolt - pump - top break - over/under - side by side - single action - double action - double action auto - muzzle loader		
Sight Type:		**Stock Type:**	
Scope Info:		**Rings/Bases:**	

Acquisition Information

Obtained From:		**Id No.:**	
Name and address		**DOB:**	
		Relationship:	
		Date Purchased:	
Price Paid:	$	**Replacement Value:**	$

Special Or Specific Information

Accessories:		**Best Load:**	
Special Marks Or Cartouches:		**Maint Info:**	
Other Notes:			

Disposition Information

If I should die I want this firearm to go to:			
Gun Sold To:		**Id No.:**	
Name and address		**DOB:**	
		Relationship:	
		Date Sold:	
Selling Price:	$	**Lost/Stolen:**	

Additional Notes:

Photo:

Personal Firearms Basic Ownership Datasheet

Firearm Type:	rifle - handgun - shotgun - airgun - black powder other:	Serial Number:	
Manufacturer:		Other Id No.:	
Caliber:		Capacity:	
Model/Type:		Weight:	
Barrel Length		Barrel Type:	Standard - Target - Bull - Other:
Finish:	Blue - Stainless - Parkerized - Plated (type): _____ other: _____		
Action: Circle all that apply	revolver - single shot - semiauto - full auto - lever - bolt - pump - top break - over/under - side by side - single action - double action - double action auto - muzzle loader		
Sight Type:		Stock Type:	
Scope Info:		Rings/Bases:	

Acquisition Information

Obtained From:		Id No.:	
Name and address		DOB:	
		Relationship:	
		Date Purchased:	
Price Paid:	$	Replacement Value:	$

Special Or Specific Information

Accessories:		Best Load:	
Special Marks Or Cartouches:		Maint Info:	
Other Notes:			

Disposition Information

If I should die I want this firearm to go to:			
Gun Sold To:		Id No.:	
Name and address		DOB:	
		Relationship:	
		Date Sold:	
Selling Price:	$	Lost/Stolen:	

Additional Notes:

Photo:

Personal Firearms Basic Ownership Datasheet

Firearm Type:	rifle - handgun - shotgun - airgun - black powder other:	Serial Number:	
Manufacturer:		Other Id No.:	
Caliber:		Capacity:	
Model/Type:		Weight:	
Barrel Length		Barrel Type:	Standard - Target - Bull - Other:
Finish:	Blue - Stainless - Parkerized - Plated (type): _____ other: _____		
Action: Circle all that apply	revolver - single shot - semiauto - full auto - lever - bolt - pump - top break - over/under - side by side - single action - double action - double action auto - muzzle loader		
Sight Type:		Stock Type:	
Scope Info:		Rings/Bases:	

Acquisition Information

Obtained From:		Id No.:	
Name and address		DOB:	
		Relationship:	
		Date Purchased:	
Price Paid:	$	Replacement Value:	$

Special Or Specific Information

Accessories:		Best Load:	
Special Marks Or Cartouches:		Maint Info:	
Other Notes:			

Disposition Information

If I should die I want this firearm to go to:

Gun Sold To:		Id No.:	
Name and address		DOB:	
		Relationship:	
		Date Sold:	
Selling Price:	$	Lost/Stolen:	

Additional Notes:

Photo:

Personal Firearms Basic Ownership Datasheet

Firearm Type:	rifle - handgun - shotgun - airgun - black powder other:	**Serial Number:**	
Manufacturer:		**Other Id No.:**	
Caliber:		**Capacity:**	
Model/Type:		**Weight:**	
Barrel Length		**Barrel Type:**	Standard - Target - Bull - Other:
Finish:	Blue - Stainless - Parkerized - Plated (type): _____ other: _____		
Action: Circle all that apply	revolver - single shot - semiauto - full auto - lever - bolt - pump - top break - over/under - side by side - single action - double action - double action auto - muzzle loader		
Sight Type:		**Stock Type:**	
Scope Info:		**Rings/Bases:**	

Acquisition Information

Obtained From:		**Id No.:**	
Name and address		**DOB:**	
		Relationship:	
		Date Purchased:	
Price Paid:	$	**Replacement Value:**	$

Special Or Specific Information

Accessories:		**Best Load:**	
Special Marks Or Cartouches:		**Maint Info:**	
Other Notes:			

Disposition Information

If I should die I want this firearm to go to:

Gun Sold To:		**Id No.:**	
Name and address		**DOB:**	
		Relationship:	
		Date Sold:	
Selling Price:	$	**Lost/Stolen:**	

Additional Notes:

Photo:

Personal Firearms Basic Ownership Datasheet

Firearm Type:	rifle - handgun - shotgun - airgun - black powder other:	**Serial Number:**	
Manufacturer:		**Other Id No.:**	
Caliber:		**Capacity:**	
Model/Type:		**Weight:**	
Barrel Length		**Barrel Type:**	Standard - Target - Bull - Other:
Finish:	Blue - Stainless - Parkerized - Plated (type): _____ other: _____		
Action: Circle all that apply	revolver - single shot - semiauto - full auto - lever - bolt - pump - top break - over/under - side by side - single action - double action - double action auto - muzzle loader		
Sight Type:		**Stock Type:**	
Scope Info:		**Rings/Bases:**	

Acquisition Information

Obtained From:		**Id No.:**	
		DOB:	
Name and address		**Relationship:**	
		Date Purchased:	
Price Paid:	$	**Replacement Value:**	$

Special Or Specific Information

Accessories:		**Best Load:**	
Special Marks Or Cartouches:		**Maint Info:**	
Other Notes:			

Disposition Information

If I should die I want this firearm to go to:			
Gun Sold To:		**Id No.:**	
		DOB:	
Name and address		**Relationship:**	
		Date Sold:	
Selling Price:	$	**Lost/Stolen:**	

Additional Notes:

Photo:

Personal Firearms Basic Ownership Datasheet

Firearm Type:	rifle - handgun - shotgun - airgun - black powder other:	**Serial Number:**	
Manufacturer:		**Other Id No.:**	
Caliber:		**Capacity:**	
Model/Type:		**Weight:**	
Barrel Length		**Barrel Type:**	Standard - Target - Bull - Other:
Finish:	Blue - Stainless - Parkerized - Plated (type): _____ other: _____		
Action: Circle all that apply	revolver - single shot - semiauto - full auto - lever - bolt - pump - top break - over/under - side by side - single action - double action - double action auto - muzzle loader		
Sight Type:		**Stock Type:**	
Scope Info:		**Rings/Bases:**	

Acquisition Information

Obtained From:		**Id No.:**	
Name and address		**DOB:**	
		Relationship:	
		Date Purchased:	
Price Paid:	$	**Replacement Value:**	$

Special Or Specific Information

Accessories:		**Best Load:**	
Special Marks Or Cartouches:		**Maint Info:**	
Other Notes:			

Disposition Information

If I should die I want this firearm to go to:

Gun Sold To:		**Id No.:**	
Name and address		**DOB:**	
		Relationship:	
		Date Sold:	
Selling Price:	$	**Lost/Stolen:**	

Additional Notes:

Photo:

Personal Firearms Basic Ownership Datasheet

Firearm Type:	rifle - handgun - shotgun - airgun - black powder other:	Serial Number:	
Manufacturer:		Other Id No.:	
Caliber:		Capacity:	
Model/Type:		Weight:	
Barrel Length		Barrel Type:	Standard - Target - Bull - Other:
Finish:	Blue - Stainless - Parkerized - Plated (type): _____ other: _____		
Action: Circle all that apply	revolver - single shot - semiauto - full auto - lever - bolt - pump - top break - over/under - side by side - single action - double action - double action auto - muzzle loader		
Sight Type:		Stock Type:	
Scope Info:		Rings/Bases:	

Acquisition Information

Obtained From:		Id No.:	
		DOB:	
Name and address		Relationship:	
		Date Purchased:	
Price Paid:	$	Replacement Value:	$

Special Or Specific Information

Accessories:		Best Load:	
Special Marks Or Cartouches:		Maint Info:	
Other Notes:			

Disposition Information

If I should die I want this firearm to go to:			
Gun Sold To:		Id No.:	
		DOB:	
Name and address		Relationship:	
		Date Sold:	
Selling Price:	$	Lost/Stolen:	

Additional Notes:

Photo:

Personal Firearms Basic Ownership Datasheet

Firearm Type:	rifle - handgun - shotgun - airgun - black powder other:	Serial Number:	
Manufacturer:		Other Id No.:	
Caliber:		Capacity:	
Model/Type:		Weight:	
Barrel Length		Barrel Type:	Standard - Target - Bull - Other:
Finish:	Blue - Stainless - Parkerized - Plated (type): _____ other: _____		
Action: Circle all that apply	revolver - single shot - semiauto - full auto - lever - bolt - pump - top break - over/under - side by side - single action - double action - double action auto - muzzle loader		
Sight Type:		Stock Type:	
Scope Info:		Rings/Bases:	

Acquisition Information

Obtained From:		Id No.:	
Name and address		DOB:	
		Relationship:	
		Date Purchased:	
Price Paid:	$	Replacement Value:	$

Special Or Specific Information

Accessories:		Best Load:	
Special Marks Or Cartouches:		Maint Info:	
Other Notes:			

Disposition Information

If I should die I want this firearm to go to:			
Gun Sold To:		Id No.:	
Name and address		DOB:	
		Relationship:	
		Date Sold:	
Selling Price:	$	Lost/Stolen:	

Additional Notes:

Photo:

Personal Firearms Basic Ownership Datasheet

Firearm Type:	rifle - handgun - shotgun - airgun - black powder other:	**Serial Number:**	
Manufacturer:		**Other Id No.:**	
Caliber:		**Capacity:**	
Model/Type:		**Weight:**	
Barrel Length		**Barrel Type:**	Standard - Target - Bull - Other:
Finish:	Blue - Stainless - Parkerized - Plated (type): _____ other: _____		
Action: Circle all that apply	revolver - single shot - semiauto - full auto - lever - bolt - pump - top break - over/under - side by side - single action - double action - double action auto - muzzle loader		
Sight Type:		**Stock Type:**	
Scope Info:		**Rings/Bases:**	

Acquisition Information

Obtained From:		**Id No.:**	
Name and address		**DOB:**	
		Relationship:	
		Date Purchased:	
Price Paid:	$	**Replacement Value:**	$

Special Or Specific Information

Accessories:		**Best Load:**	
Special Marks Or Cartouches:		**Maint Info:**	
Other Notes:			

Disposition Information

If I should die I want this firearm to go to:			
Gun Sold To:		**Id No.:**	
Name and address		**DOB:**	
		Relationship:	
		Date Sold:	
Selling Price:	$	**Lost/Stolen:**	

Additional Notes:

Photo:

Personal Firearms Basic Ownership Datasheet

Firearm Type:	rifle - handgun - shotgun - airgun - black powder other:	**Serial Number:**	
Manufacturer:		**Other Id No.:**	
Caliber:		**Capacity:**	
Model/Type:		**Weight:**	
Barrel Length		**Barrel Type:**	Standard - Target - Bull - Other:
Finish:	Blue - Stainless - Parkerized - Plated (type): _____ other: _____		
Action: Circle all that apply	revolver - single shot - semiauto - full auto - lever - bolt - pump - top break - over/under - side by side - single action - double action - double action auto - muzzle loader		
Sight Type:		**Stock Type:**	
Scope Info:		**Rings/Bases:**	

Acquisition Information

Obtained From:		**Id No.:**	
Name and address		**DOB:**	
		Relationship:	
		Date Purchased:	
Price Paid:	$	**Replacement Value:**	$

Special Or Specific Information

Accessories:		**Best Load:**	
Special Marks Or Cartouches:		**Maint Info:**	
Other Notes:			

Disposition Information

If I should die I want this firearm to go to:			
Gun Sold To:		**Id No.:**	
Name and address		**DOB:**	
		Relationship:	
		Date Sold:	
Selling Price:	$	**Lost/Stolen:**	

Additional Notes:

Photo:

Personal Firearms Basic Ownership Datasheet

Firearm Type:	rifle - handgun - shotgun - airgun - black powder other:	Serial Number:	
Manufacturer:		Other Id No.:	
Caliber:		Capacity:	
Model/Type:		Weight:	
Barrel Length		Barrel Type:	Standard - Target - Bull - Other:
Finish:	Blue - Stainless - Parkerized - Plated (type): _____ other: _____		
Action: Circle all that apply	revolver - single shot - semiauto - full auto - lever - bolt - pump - top break - over/under - side by side - single action - double action - double action auto - muzzle loader		
Sight Type:		Stock Type:	
Scope Info:		Rings/Bases:	

Acquisition Information

Obtained From:		Id No.:	
Name and address		DOB:	
		Relationship:	
		Date Purchased:	
Price Paid:	$	Replacement Value:	$

Special Or Specific Information

Accessories:		Best Load:	
Special Marks Or Cartouches:		Maint Info:	
Other Notes:			

Disposition Information

If I should die I want this firearm to go to:			
Gun Sold To:		Id No.:	
Name and address		DOB:	
		Relationship:	
		Date Sold:	
Selling Price:	$	Lost/Stolen:	

Additional Notes:

Photo:

Personal Firearms Basic Ownership Datasheet

Firearm Type:	rifle - handgun - shotgun - airgun - black powder other:	**Serial Number:**	
Manufacturer:		**Other Id No.:**	
Caliber:		**Capacity:**	
Model/Type:		**Weight:**	
Barrel Length		**Barrel Type:**	Standard - Target - Bull - Other:
Finish:	Blue - Stainless - Parkerized - Plated (type): _____ other: _____		
Action: Circle all that apply	revolver - single shot - semiauto - full auto - lever - bolt - pump - top break - over/under - side by side - single action - double action - double action auto - muzzle loader		
Sight Type:		**Stock Type:**	
Scope Info:		**Rings/Bases:**	

Acquisition Information

Obtained From:		**Id No.:**	
Name and address		**DOB:**	
		Relationship:	
		Date Purchased:	
Price Paid:	$	**Replacement Value:**	$

Special Or Specific Information

Accessories:		**Best Load:**	
Special Marks Or Cartouches:		**Maint Info:**	
Other Notes:			

Disposition Information

If I should die I want this firearm to go to:			
Gun Sold To:		**Id No.:**	
Name and address		**DOB:**	
		Relationship:	
		Date Sold:	
Selling Price:	$	**Lost/Stolen:**	

Additional Notes:

Photo:

Personal Firearms Basic Ownership Datasheet

Firearm Type:	rifle - handgun - shotgun - airgun - black powder other:	Serial Number:	
Manufacturer:		Other Id No.:	
Caliber:		Capacity:	
Model/Type:		Weight:	
Barrel Length		Barrel Type:	Standard - Target - Bull - Other:
Finish:	Blue - Stainless - Parkerized - Plated (type): _____ other: _____		
Action: Circle all that apply	revolver - single shot - semiauto - full auto - lever - bolt - pump - top break - over/under - side by side - single action - double action - double action auto - muzzle loader		
Sight Type:		Stock Type:	
Scope Info:		Rings/Bases:	

Acquisition Information

Obtained From:		Id No.:	
Name and address		DOB:	
		Relationship:	
		Date Purchased:	
Price Paid:	$	Replacement Value:	$

Special Or Specific Information

Accessories:		Best Load:	
Special Marks Or Cartouches:		Maint Info:	
Other Notes:			

Disposition Information

If I should die I want this firearm to go to:			
Gun Sold To:		Id No.:	
Name and address		DOB:	
		Relationship:	
		Date Sold:	
Selling Price:	$	Lost/Stolen:	

Additional Notes:

Photo:

Personal Firearms Basic Ownership Datasheet

Firearm Type:	rifle - handgun - shotgun - airgun - black powder other:	**Serial Number:**	
Manufacturer:		**Other Id No.:**	
Caliber:		**Capacity:**	
Model/Type:		**Weight:**	
Barrel Length		**Barrel Type:**	Standard - Target - Bull - Other:
Finish:	Blue - Stainless - Parkerized - Plated (type): _____ other: _____		
Action: Circle all that apply	revolver - single shot - semiauto - full auto - lever - bolt - pump - top break - over/under - side by side - single action - double action - double action auto - muzzle loader		
Sight Type:		**Stock Type:**	
Scope Info:		**Rings/Bases:**	

Acquisition Information

Obtained From:		**Id No.:**	
Name and address		**DOB:**	
		Relationship:	
		Date Purchased:	
Price Paid:	$	**Replacement Value:**	$

Special Or Specific Information

Accessories:		**Best Load:**	
Special Marks Or Cartouches:		**Maint Info:**	
Other Notes:			

Disposition Information

If I should die I want this firearm to go to:

Gun Sold To:		**Id No.:**	
Name and address		**DOB:**	
		Relationship:	
		Date Sold:	
Selling Price:	$	**Lost/Stolen:**	

Additional Notes:

Photo:

Personal Firearms Basic Ownership Datasheet

Firearm Type:	rifle - handgun - shotgun - airgun - black powder other:	**Serial Number:**	
Manufacturer:		**Other Id No.:**	
Caliber:		**Capacity:**	
Model/Type:		**Weight:**	
Barrel Length		**Barrel Type:**	Standard - Target - Bull - Other:
Finish:	Blue - Stainless - Parkerized - Plated (type): _____ other: _____		
Action: Circle all that apply	revolver - single shot - semiauto - full auto - lever - bolt - pump - top break - over/under - side by side - single action - double action - double action auto - muzzle loader		
Sight Type:		**Stock Type:**	
Scope Info:		**Rings/Bases:**	

Acquisition Information

Obtained From:		**Id No.:**	
Name and address		**DOB:**	
		Relationship:	
		Date Purchased:	
Price Paid:	$	**Replacement Value:**	$

Special Or Specific Information

Accessories:		**Best Load:**	
Special Marks Or Cartouches:		**Maint Info:**	
Other Notes:			

Disposition Information

If I should die I want this firearm to go to:			
Gun Sold To:		**Id No.:**	
Name and address		**DOB:**	
		Relationship:	
		Date Sold:	
Selling Price:	$	**Lost/Stolen:**	

Additional Notes:

Photo:

Personal Firearms Basic Ownership Datasheet

Firearm Type:	rifle - handgun - shotgun - airgun - black powder other:	Serial Number:	
Manufacturer:		Other Id No.:	
Caliber:		Capacity:	
Model/Type:		Weight:	
Barrel Length		Barrel Type:	Standard - Target - Bull - Other:
Finish:	Blue - Stainless - Parkerized - Plated (type): _____ other: _____		
Action: Circle all that apply	revolver - single shot - semiauto - full auto - lever - bolt - pump - top break - over/under - side by side - single action - double action - double action auto - muzzle loader		
Sight Type:		Stock Type:	
Scope Info:		Rings/Bases:	

Acquisition Information

Obtained From:		Id No.:	
Name and address		DOB:	
		Relationship:	
		Date Purchased:	
Price Paid:	$	Replacement Value:	$

Special Or Specific Information

Accessories:		Best Load:	
Special Marks Or Cartouches:		Maint Info:	
Other Notes:			

Disposition Information

If I should die I want this firearm to go to:			
Gun Sold To:		Id No.:	
Name and address		DOB:	
		Relationship:	
		Date Sold:	
Selling Price:	$	Lost/Stolen:	

Additional Notes:

Photo:

Personal Firearms Basic Ownership Datasheet

Firearm Type:	rifle - handgun - shotgun - airgun - black powder other:	Serial Number:	
Manufacturer:		Other Id No.:	
Caliber:		Capacity:	
Model/Type:		Weight:	
Barrel Length		Barrel Type:	Standard - Target - Bull - Other:
Finish:	Blue - Stainless - Parkerized - Plated (type): _____ other: _____		
Action: Circle all that apply	revolver - single shot - semiauto - full auto - lever - bolt - pump - top break - over/under - side by side - single action - double action - double action auto - muzzle loader		
Sight Type:		Stock Type:	
Scope Info:		Rings/Bases:	

Acquisition Information

Obtained From:		Id No.:	
Name and address		DOB:	
		Relationship:	
		Date Purchased:	
Price Paid:	$	Replacement Value:	$

Special Or Specific Information

Accessories:		Best Load:	
Special Marks Or Cartouches:		Maint Info:	
Other Notes:			

Disposition Information

If I should die I want this firearm to go to:

Gun Sold To:		Id No.:	
Name and address		DOB:	
		Relationship:	
		Date Sold:	
Selling Price:	$	Lost/Stolen:	

Additional Notes:

Photo:

Personal Firearms Basic Ownership Datasheet

Firearm Type:	rifle - handgun - shotgun - airgun - black powder other:	Serial Number:	
Manufacturer:		Other Id No.:	
Caliber:		Capacity:	
Model/Type:		Weight:	
Barrel Length		Barrel Type:	Standard - Target - Bull - Other:
Finish:	Blue - Stainless - Parkerized - Plated (type): _____ other: _____		
Action: Circle all that apply	revolver - single shot - semiauto - full auto - lever - bolt - pump - top break - over/under - side by side - single action - double action - double action auto - muzzle loader		
Sight Type:		Stock Type:	
Scope Info:		Rings/Bases:	

Acquisition Information

Obtained From:		Id No.:	
Name and address		DOB:	
		Relationship:	
		Date Purchased:	
Price Paid:	$	Replacement Value:	$

Special Or Specific Information

Accessories:		Best Load:	
Special Marks Or Cartouches:		Maint Info:	
Other Notes:			

Disposition Information

If I should die I want this firearm to go to:			
Gun Sold To:		Id No.:	
Name and address		DOB:	
		Relationship:	
		Date Sold:	
Selling Price:	$	Lost/Stolen:	

Additional Notes:

Photo:

Personal Firearms Basic Ownership Datasheet

Firearm Type:	rifle - handgun - shotgun - airgun - black powder other:	**Serial Number:**	
Manufacturer:		**Other Id No.:**	
Caliber:		**Capacity:**	
Model/Type:		**Weight:**	
Barrel Length		**Barrel Type:**	Standard - Target - Bull - Other:
Finish:	Blue - Stainless - Parkerized - Plated (type): _____ other: _____		
Action: Circle all that apply	revolver - single shot - semiauto - full auto - lever - bolt - pump - top break - over/under - side by side - single action - double action - double action auto - muzzle loader		
Sight Type:		**Stock Type:**	
Scope Info:		**Rings/Bases:**	

Acquisition Information

Obtained From:		**Id No.:**	
Name and address		**DOB:**	
		Relationship:	
		Date Purchased:	
Price Paid:	$	**Replacement Value:**	$

Special Or Specific Information

Accessories:		**Best Load:**	
Special Marks Or Cartouches:		**Maint Info:**	
Other Notes:			

Disposition Information

If I should die I want this firearm to go to:

Gun Sold To:		**Id No.:**	
Name and address		**DOB:**	
		Relationship:	
		Date Sold:	
Selling Price:	$	**Lost/Stolen:**	

Additional Notes:

Photo:

Personal Firearms Basic Ownership Datasheet

Firearm Type:	rifle - handgun - shotgun - airgun - black powder other:	Serial Number:	
Manufacturer:		Other Id No.:	
Caliber:		Capacity:	
Model/Type:		Weight:	
Barrel Length		Barrel Type:	Standard - Target - Bull - Other:
Finish:	Blue - Stainless - Parkerized - Plated (type): _____ other: _____		
Action: Circle all that apply	revolver - single shot - semiauto - full auto - lever - bolt - pump - top break - over/under - side by side - single action - double action - double action auto - muzzle loader		
Sight Type:		Stock Type:	
Scope Info:		Rings/Bases:	

Acquisition Information

Obtained From:		Id No.:	
Name and address		DOB:	
		Relationship:	
		Date Purchased:	
Price Paid:	$	Replacement Value:	$

Special Or Specific Information

Accessories:		Best Load:	
Special Marks Or Cartouches:		Maint Info:	
Other Notes:			

Disposition Information

If I should die I want this firearm to go to:			
Gun Sold To:		Id No.:	
Name and address		DOB:	
		Relationship:	
		Date Sold:	
Selling Price:	$	Lost/Stolen:	

Additional Notes:

Photo:

Personal Firearms Basic Ownership Datasheet

Firearm Type:	rifle - handgun - shotgun - airgun - black powder other:	**Serial Number:**	
Manufacturer:		**Other Id No.:**	
Caliber:		**Capacity:**	
Model/Type:		**Weight:**	
Barrel Length		**Barrel Type:**	Standard - Target - Bull - Other:
Finish:	Blue - Stainless - Parkerized - Plated (type): _____ other: _____		
Action: Circle all that apply	revolver - single shot - semiauto - full auto - lever - bolt - pump - top break - over/under - side by side - single action - double action - double action auto - muzzle loader		
Sight Type:		**Stock Type:**	
Scope Info:		**Rings/Bases:**	

Acquisition Information

Obtained From:		**Id No.:**	
Name and address		**DOB:**	
		Relationship:	
		Date Purchased:	
Price Paid:	$	**Replacement Value:**	$

Special Or Specific Information

Accessories:		**Best Load:**	
Special Marks Or Cartouches:		**Maint Info:**	
Other Notes:			

Disposition Information

If I should die I want this firearm to go to:

Gun Sold To:		**Id No.:**	
Name and address		**DOB:**	
		Relationship:	
		Date Sold:	
Selling Price:	$	**Lost/Stolen:**	

Additional Notes:

Photo:

Personal Firearms Basic Ownership Datasheet

Firearm Type:	rifle - handgun - shotgun - airgun - black powder other:	**Serial Number:**	
Manufacturer:		**Other Id No.:**	
Caliber:		**Capacity:**	
Model/Type:		**Weight:**	
Barrel Length		**Barrel Type:**	Standard - Target - Bull - Other:
Finish:	Blue - Stainless - Parkerized - Plated (type): _____ other: _____		
Action: Circle all that apply	revolver - single shot - semiauto - full auto - lever - bolt - pump - top break - over/under - side by side - single action - double action - double action auto - muzzle loader		
Sight Type:		**Stock Type:**	
Scope Info:		**Rings/Bases:**	

Acquisition Information

Obtained From:		**Id No.:**	
		DOB:	
Name and address		**Relationship:**	
		Date Purchased:	
Price Paid:	$	**Replacement Value:**	$

Special Or Specific Information

Accessories:		**Best Load:**	
Special Marks Or Cartouches:		**Maint Info:**	
Other Notes:			

Disposition Information

If I should die I want this firearm to go to:			
Gun Sold To:		**Id No.:**	
		DOB:	
Name and address		**Relationship:**	
		Date Sold:	
Selling Price:	$	**Lost/Stolen:**	

Additional Notes:

Photo:

Personal Firearms Basic Ownership Datasheet

Firearm Type:	rifle - handgun - shotgun - airgun - black powder other:	Serial Number:	
Manufacturer:		Other Id No.:	
Caliber:		Capacity:	
Model/Type:		Weight:	
Barrel Length:		Barrel Type:	Standard - Target - Bull - Other:
Finish:	Blue - Stainless - Parkerized - Plated (type): _____ other: _____		
Action: Circle all that apply	revolver - single shot - semiauto - full auto - lever - bolt - pump - top break - over/under - side by side - single action - double action - double action auto - muzzle loader		
Sight Type:		Stock Type:	
Scope Info:		Rings/Bases:	

Acquisition Information

Obtained From:		Id No.:	
Name and address		DOB:	
		Relationship:	
		Date Purchased:	
Price Paid:	$	Replacement Value:	$

Special Or Specific Information

Accessories:		Best Load:	
Special Marks Or Cartouches:		Maint Info:	
Other Notes:			

Disposition Information

If I should die I want this firearm to go to:			
Gun Sold To:		Id No.:	
Name and address		DOB:	
		Relationship:	
		Date Sold:	
Selling Price:	$	Lost/Stolen:	

Additional Notes:

Photo:

Personal Firearms Basic Ownership Datasheet

Firearm Type:	rifle - handgun - shotgun - airgun - black powder other:	Serial Number:	
Manufacturer:		Other Id No.:	
Caliber:		Capacity:	
Model/Type:		Weight:	
Barrel Length		Barrel Type:	Standard - Target - Bull - Other:
Finish:	Blue - Stainless - Parkerized - Plated (type): _____ other: _____		
Action: Circle all that apply	revolver - single shot - semiauto - full auto - lever - bolt - pump - top break - over/under - side by side - single action - double action - double action auto - muzzle loader		
Sight Type:		Stock Type:	
Scope Info:		Rings/Bases:	

Acquisition Information

Obtained From:		Id No.:	
Name and address		DOB:	
		Relationship:	
		Date Purchased:	
Price Paid:	$	Replacement Value:	$

Special Or Specific Information

Accessories:		Best Load:	
Special Marks Or Cartouches:		Maint Info:	
Other Notes:			

Disposition Information

If I should die I want this firearm to go to:

Gun Sold To:		Id No.:	
Name and address		DOB:	
		Relationship:	
		Date Sold:	
Selling Price:	$	Lost/Stolen:	

Additional Notes:

Photo:

Personal Firearms Basic Ownership Datasheet

Firearm Type:	rifle - handgun - shotgun - airgun - black powder other:	**Serial Number:**	
Manufacturer:		**Other Id No.:**	
Caliber:		**Capacity:**	
Model/Type:		**Weight:**	
Barrel Length		**Barrel Type:**	Standard - Target - Bull - Other:
Finish:	Blue - Stainless - Parkerized - Plated (type): _____ other: _____		
Action: Circle all that apply	revolver - single shot - semiauto - full auto - lever - bolt - pump - top break - over/under - side by side - single action - double action - double action auto - muzzle loader		
Sight Type:		**Stock Type:**	
Scope Info:		**Rings/Bases:**	

Acquisition Information

Obtained From:		**Id No.:**	
		DOB:	
Name and address		**Relationship:**	
		Date Purchased:	
Price Paid:	$	**Replacement Value:**	$

Special Or Specific Information

Accessories:		**Best Load:**	
Special Marks Or Cartouches:		**Maint Info:**	
Other Notes:			

Disposition Information

If I should die I want this firearm to go to:

Gun Sold To:		**Id No.:**	
		DOB:	
Name and address		**Relationship:**	
		Date Sold:	
Selling Price:	$	**Lost/Stolen:**	

Additional Notes:

Photo:

Personal Firearms Basic Ownership Datasheet

Firearm Type:	rifle - handgun - shotgun - airgun - black powder other:	**Serial Number:**	
Manufacturer:		**Other Id No.:**	
Caliber:		**Capacity:**	
Model/Type:		**Weight:**	
Barrel Length		**Barrel Type:**	Standard - Target - Bull - Other:
Finish:	Blue - Stainless - Parkerized - Plated (type): _____ other: _____		
Action: Circle all that apply	revolver - single shot - semiauto - full auto - lever - bolt - pump - top break - over/under - side by side - single action - double action - double action auto - muzzle loader		
Sight Type:		**Stock Type:**	
Scope Info:		**Rings/Bases:**	

Acquisition Information

Obtained From:		**Id No.:**	
Name and address		**DOB:**	
		Relationship:	
		Date Purchased:	
Price Paid:	$	**Replacement Value:**	$

Special Or Specific Information

Accessories:		**Best Load:**	
Special Marks Or Cartouches:		**Maint Info:**	
Other Notes:			

Disposition Information

If I should die I want this firearm to go to:

Gun Sold To:		**Id No.:**	
Name and address		**DOB:**	
		Relationship:	
		Date Sold:	
Selling Price:	$	**Lost/Stolen:**	

Additional Notes:

Photo:

Personal Firearms Basic Ownership Datasheet

Firearm Type:	rifle - handgun - shotgun - airgun - black powder other:	**Serial Number:**	
Manufacturer:		**Other Id No.:**	
Caliber:		**Capacity:**	
Model/Type:		**Weight:**	
Barrel Length		**Barrel Type:**	Standard - Target - Bull - Other:
Finish:	Blue - Stainless - Parkerized - Plated (type): _____ other: _____		
Action: Circle all that apply	revolver - single shot - semiauto - full auto - lever - bolt - pump - top break - over/under - side by side - single action - double action - double action auto - muzzle loader		
Sight Type:		**Stock Type:**	
Scope Info:		**Rings/Bases:**	

Acquisition Information

Obtained From:		**Id No.:**	
Name and address		**DOB:**	
		Relationship:	
		Date Purchased:	
Price Paid:	$	**Replacement Value:**	$

Special Or Specific Information

Accessories:		**Best Load:**	
Special Marks Or Cartouches:		**Maint Info:**	
Other Notes:			

Disposition Information

If I should die I want this firearm to go to:

Gun Sold To:		**Id No.:**	
Name and address		**DOB:**	
		Relationship:	
		Date Sold:	
Selling Price:	$	**Lost/Stolen:**	

Additional Notes:

Photo:

Personal Firearms Basic Ownership Datasheet

Firearm Type:	rifle - handgun - shotgun - airgun - black powder other:	**Serial Number:**	
Manufacturer:		**Other Id No.:**	
Caliber:		**Capacity:**	
Model/Type:		**Weight:**	
Barrel Length		**Barrel Type:**	Standard - Target - Bull - Other:
Finish:	Blue - Stainless - Parkerized - Plated (type): _____ other: _____		
Action: Circle all that apply	revolver - single shot - semiauto - full auto - lever - bolt - pump - top break - over/under - side by side - single action - double action - double action auto - muzzle loader		
Sight Type:		**Stock Type:**	
Scope Info:		**Rings/Bases:**	

Acquisition Information

Obtained From:		**Id No.:**	
Name and address		**DOB:**	
		Relationship:	
		Date Purchased:	
Price Paid:	$	**Replacement Value:**	$

Special Or Specific Information

Accessories:		**Best Load:**	
Special Marks Or Cartouches:		**Maint Info:**	
Other Notes:			

Disposition Information

If I should die I want this firearm to go to:			
Gun Sold To:		**Id No.:**	
Name and address		**DOB:**	
		Relationship:	
		Date Sold:	
Selling Price:	$	**Lost/Stolen:**	

Additional Notes:

Photo:

Personal Firearms Basic Ownership Datasheet

Firearm Type:	rifle - handgun - shotgun - airgun - black powder other:	Serial Number:	
Manufacturer:		Other Id No.:	
Caliber:		Capacity:	
Model/Type:		Weight:	
Barrel Length		Barrel Type:	Standard - Target - Bull - Other:
Finish:	Blue - Stainless - Parkerized - Plated (type): _____ other: _____		
Action: Circle all that apply	revolver - single shot - semiauto - full auto - lever - bolt - pump - top break - over/under - side by side - single action - double action - double action auto - muzzle loader		
Sight Type:		Stock Type:	
Scope Info:		Rings/Bases:	

Acquisition Information

Obtained From:		Id No.:	
Name and address		DOB:	
		Relationship:	
		Date Purchased:	
Price Paid:	$	Replacement Value:	$

Special Or Specific Information

Accessories:		Best Load:	
Special Marks Or Cartouches:		Maint Info:	
Other Notes:			

Disposition Information

If I should die I want this firearm to go to:

Gun Sold To:		Id No.:	
Name and address		DOB:	
		Relationship:	
		Date Sold:	
Selling Price:	$	Lost/Stolen:	

Additional Notes:

Photo:

Personal Firearms Basic Ownership Datasheet

Firearm Type:	rifle - handgun - shotgun - airgun - black powder other:	Serial Number:	
Manufacturer:		Other Id No.:	
Caliber:		Capacity:	
Model/Type:		Weight:	
Barrel Length		Barrel Type:	Standard - Target - Bull - Other:
Finish:	Blue - Stainless - Parkerized - Plated (type): _____ other: _____		
Action: Circle all that apply	revolver - single shot - semiauto - full auto - lever - bolt - pump - top break - over/under - side by side - single action - double action - double action auto - muzzle loader		
Sight Type:		Stock Type:	
Scope Info:		Rings/Bases:	

Acquisition Information

Obtained From:		Id No.:	
Name and address		DOB:	
		Relationship:	
		Date Purchased:	
Price Paid:	$	Replacement Value:	$

Special Or Specific Information

Accessories:		Best Load:	
Special Marks Or Cartouches:		Maint Info:	
Other Notes:			

Disposition Information

If I should die I want this firearm to go to:

Gun Sold To:		Id No.:	
Name and address		DOB:	
		Relationship:	
		Date Sold:	
Selling Price:	$	Lost/Stolen:	

Additional Notes:

Photo:

Personal Firearms Basic Ownership Datasheet

Firearm Type:	rifle - handgun - shotgun - airgun - black powder other:	**Serial Number:**	
Manufacturer:		**Other Id No.:**	
Caliber:		**Capacity:**	
Model/Type:		**Weight:**	
Barrel Length		**Barrel Type:**	Standard - Target - Bull - Other:
Finish:	Blue - Stainless - Parkerized - Plated (type): _____ other: _____		
Action: Circle all that apply	revolver - single shot - semiauto - full auto - lever - bolt - pump - top break - over/under - side by side - single action - double action - double action auto - muzzle loader		
Sight Type:		**Stock Type:**	
Scope Info:		**Rings/Bases:**	

Acquisition Information

Obtained From:		**Id No.:**	
Name and address		**DOB:**	
		Relationship:	
		Date Purchased:	
Price Paid:	$	**Replacement Value:**	$

Special Or Specific Information

Accessories:		**Best Load:**	
Special Marks Or Cartouches:		**Maint Info:**	
Other Notes:			

Disposition Information

If I should die I want this firearm to go to:

Gun Sold To:		**Id No.:**	
Name and address		**DOB:**	
		Relationship:	
		Date Sold:	
Selling Price:	$	**Lost/Stolen:**	

Additional Notes:

Photo:

Personal Firearms Basic Ownership Datasheet

Firearm Type:	rifle - handgun - shotgun - airgun - black powder other:	Serial Number:	
Manufacturer:		Other Id No.:	
Caliber:		Capacity:	
Model/Type:		Weight:	
Barrel Length		Barrel Type:	Standard - Target - Bull - Other:
Finish:	Blue - Stainless - Parkerized - Plated (type): _____ other: _____		
Action: Circle all that apply	revolver - single shot - semiauto - full auto - lever - bolt - pump - top break - over/under - side by side - single action - double action - double action auto - muzzle loader		
Sight Type:		Stock Type:	
Scope Info:		Rings/Bases:	

Acquisition Information

Obtained From:		Id No.:	
Name and address		DOB:	
		Relationship:	
		Date Purchased:	
Price Paid:	$	Replacement Value:	$

Special Or Specific Information

Accessories:		Best Load:	
Special Marks Or Cartouches:		Maint Info:	
Other Notes:			

Disposition Information

If I should die I want this firearm to go to:

Gun Sold To:		Id No.:	
Name and address		DOB:	
		Relationship:	
		Date Sold:	
Selling Price:	$	Lost/Stolen:	

Additional Notes:

Photo:

Personal Firearms Basic Ownership Datasheet

Firearm Type:	rifle - handgun - shotgun - airgun - black powder other:	Serial Number:	
Manufacturer:		Other Id No.:	
Caliber:		Capacity:	
Model/Type:		Weight:	
Barrel Length		Barrel Type:	Standard - Target - Bull - Other:
Finish:	Blue - Stainless - Parkerized - Plated (type): _____ other: _____		
Action: Circle all that apply	revolver - single shot - semiauto - full auto - lever - bolt - pump - top break - over/under - side by side - single action - double action - double action auto - muzzle loader		
Sight Type:		Stock Type:	
Scope Info:		Rings/Bases:	

Acquisition Information

Obtained From:		Id No.:	
Name and address		DOB:	
		Relationship:	
		Date Purchased:	
Price Paid:	$	Replacement Value:	$

Special Or Specific Information

Accessories:		Best Load:	
Special Marks Or Cartouches:		Maint Info:	
Other Notes:			

Disposition Information

If I should die I want this firearm to go to:

Gun Sold To:		Id No.:	
Name and address		DOB:	
		Relationship:	
		Date Sold:	
Selling Price:	$	Lost/Stolen:	

Additional Notes:

Photo:

Personal Firearms Basic Ownership Datasheet

Firearm Type:	rifle - handgun - shotgun - airgun - black powder other:	**Serial Number:**	
Manufacturer:		**Other Id No.:**	
Caliber:		**Capacity:**	
Model/Type:		**Weight:**	
Barrel Length		**Barrel Type:**	Standard - Target - Bull - Other:
Finish:	Blue - Stainless - Parkerized - Plated (type): _____ other: _____		
Action: Circle all that apply	revolver - single shot - semiauto - full auto - lever - bolt - pump - top break - over/under - side by side - single action - double action - double action auto - muzzle loader		
Sight Type:		**Stock Type:**	
Scope Info:		**Rings/Bases:**	

Acquisition Information

Obtained From:		**Id No.:**	
		DOB:	
Name and address		**Relationship:**	
		Date Purchased:	
Price Paid:	$	**Replacement Value:**	$

Special Or Specific Information

Accessories:		**Best Load:**	
Special Marks Or Cartouches:		**Maint Info:**	
Other Notes:			

Disposition Information

If I should die I want this firearm to go to:

Gun Sold To:		**Id No.:**	
		DOB:	
Name and address		**Relationship:**	
		Date Sold:	
Selling Price:	$	**Lost/Stolen:**	

Additional Notes:

Photo:

Personal Firearms Basic Ownership Datasheet

Firearm Type:	rifle - handgun - shotgun - airgun - black powder other:	Serial Number:	
Manufacturer:		Other Id No.:	
Caliber:		Capacity:	
Model/Type:		Weight:	
Barrel Length		Barrel Type:	Standard - Target - Bull - Other:
Finish:	Blue - Stainless - Parkerized - Plated (type): _____ other: _____		
Action: Circle all that apply	revolver - single shot - semiauto - full auto - lever - bolt - pump - top break - over/under - side by side - single action - double action - double action auto - muzzle loader		
Sight Type:		Stock Type:	
Scope Info:		Rings/Bases:	

Acquisition Information

Obtained From:		Id No.:	
Name and address		DOB:	
		Relationship:	
		Date Purchased:	
Price Paid:	$	Replacement Value:	$

Special Or Specific Information

Accessories:		Best Load:	
Special Marks Or Cartouches:		Maint Info:	
Other Notes:			

Disposition Information

If I should die I want this firearm to go to:			
Gun Sold To:		Id No.:	
Name and address		DOB:	
		Relationship:	
		Date Sold:	
Selling Price:	$	Lost/Stolen:	

Additional Notes:

Photo:

Personal Firearms Basic Ownership Datasheet

Firearm Type:	rifle - handgun - shotgun - airgun - black powder other:	**Serial Number:**	
Manufacturer:		**Other Id No.:**	
Caliber:		**Capacity:**	
Model/Type:		**Weight:**	
Barrel Length		**Barrel Type:**	Standard - Target - Bull - Other:
Finish:	Blue - Stainless - Parkerized - Plated (type): _____ other: _____		
Action: Circle all that apply	revolver - single shot - semiauto - full auto - lever - bolt - pump - top break - over/under - side by side - single action - double action - double action auto - muzzle loader		
Sight Type:		**Stock Type:**	
Scope Info:		**Rings/Bases:**	

Acquisition Information

Obtained From:		**Id No.:**	
Name and address		**DOB:**	
		Relationship:	
		Date Purchased:	
Price Paid:	$	**Replacement Value:**	$

Special Or Specific Information

Accessories:		**Best Load:**	
Special Marks Or Cartouches:		**Maint Info:**	
Other Notes:			

Disposition Information

If I should die I want this firearm to go to:

Gun Sold To:		**Id No.:**	
Name and address		**DOB:**	
		Relationship:	
		Date Sold:	
Selling Price:	$	**Lost/Stolen:**	

Additional Notes:

Photo:

Personal Firearms Basic Ownership Datasheet			
Firearm Type:	rifle - handgun - shotgun - airgun - black powder other:	**Serial Number:**	
Manufacturer:		**Other Id No.:**	
Caliber:		**Capacity:**	
Model/Type:		**Weight:**	
Barrel Length		**Barrel Type:**	Standard - Target - Bull - Other:
Finish:	Blue - Stainless - Parkerized - Plated (type): _____ other: _____		
Action: Circle all that apply	revolver - single shot - semiauto - full auto - lever - bolt - pump - top break - over/under - side by side - single action - double action - double action auto - muzzle loader		
Sight Type:		**Stock Type:**	
Scope Info:		**Rings/Bases:**	
Acquisition Information			
Obtained From:		**Id No.:**	
Name and address		**DOB:**	
^		**Relationship:**	
^		**Date Purchased:**	
Price Paid:	$	**Replacement Value:**	$
Special Or Specific Information			
Accessories:		**Best Load:**	
Special Marks Or Cartouches:		**Maint Info:**	
Other Notes:			
Disposition Information			
If I should die I want this firearm to go to:			
Gun Sold To:		**Id No.:**	
Name and address		**DOB:**	
^		**Relationship:**	
^		**Date Sold:**	
Selling Price:	$	**Lost/Stolen:**	

Additional Notes:

Photo:

Personal Firearms Basic Ownership Datasheet

Firearm Type:	rifle - handgun - shotgun - airgun - black powder other:	Serial Number:	
Manufacturer:		Other Id No.:	
Caliber:		Capacity:	
Model/Type:		Weight:	
Barrel Length		Barrel Type:	Standard - Target - Bull - Other:
Finish:	Blue - Stainless - Parkerized - Plated (type): _____ other: _____		
Action: Circle all that apply	revolver - single shot - semiauto - full auto - lever - bolt - pump - top break - over/under - side by side - single action - double action - double action auto - muzzle loader		
Sight Type:		Stock Type:	
Scope Info:		Rings/Bases:	

Acquisition Information

Obtained From:		Id No.:	
Name and address		DOB:	
		Relationship:	
		Date Purchased:	
Price Paid:	$	Replacement Value:	$

Special Or Specific Information

Accessories:		Best Load:	
Special Marks Or Cartouches:		Maint Info:	
Other Notes:			

Disposition Information

If I should die I want this firearm to go to:			
Gun Sold To:		Id No.:	
Name and address		DOB:	
		Relationship:	
		Date Sold:	
Selling Price:	$	Lost/Stolen:	

Additional Notes:

Photo:

Personal Firearms Basic Ownership Datasheet

Firearm Type:	rifle - handgun - shotgun - airgun - black powder other:	**Serial Number:**	
Manufacturer:		**Other Id No.:**	
Caliber:		**Capacity:**	
Model/Type:		**Weight:**	
Barrel Length		**Barrel Type:**	Standard - Target - Bull - Other:
Finish:	Blue - Stainless - Parkerized - Plated (type): _____ other: _____		
Action: Circle all that apply	revolver - single shot - semiauto - full auto - lever - bolt - pump - top break - over/under - side by side - single action - double action - double action auto - muzzle loader		
Sight Type:		**Stock Type:**	
Scope Info:		**Rings/Bases:**	

Acquisition Information

Obtained From:		**Id No.:**	
		DOB:	
Name and address		**Relationship:**	
		Date Purchased:	
Price Paid:	$	**Replacement Value:**	$

Special Or Specific Information

Accessories:		**Best Load:**	
Special Marks Or Cartouches:		**Maint Info:**	
Other Notes:			

Disposition Information

If I should die I want this firearm to go to:

Gun Sold To:		**Id No.:**	
		DOB:	
Name and address		**Relationship:**	
		Date Sold:	
Selling Price:	$	**Lost/Stolen:**	

Additional Notes:

Photo:

Personal Firearms Basic Ownership Datasheet

Firearm Type:	rifle - handgun - shotgun - airgun - black powder other:	**Serial Number:**	
Manufacturer:		**Other Id No.:**	
Caliber:		**Capacity:**	
Model/Type:		**Weight:**	
Barrel Length		**Barrel Type:**	Standard - Target - Bull - Other:
Finish:	Blue - Stainless - Parkerized - Plated (type): _____ other: _____		
Action: Circle all that apply	revolver - single shot - semiauto - full auto - lever - bolt - pump - top break - over/under - side by side - single action - double action - double action auto - muzzle loader		
Sight Type:		**Stock Type:**	
Scope Info:		**Rings/Bases:**	

Acquisition Information

Obtained From:		**Id No.:**	
		DOB:	
Name and address		**Relationship:**	
		Date Purchased:	
Price Paid:	$	**Replacement Value:**	$

Special Or Specific Information

Accessories:		**Best Load:**	
Special Marks Or Cartouches:		**Maint Info:**	
Other Notes:			

Disposition Information

If I should die I want this firearm to go to:

Gun Sold To:		**Id No.:**	
		DOB:	
Name and address		**Relationship:**	
		Date Sold:	
Selling Price:	$	**Lost/Stolen:**	

Additional Notes:

Photo:

Personal Firearms Basic Ownership Datasheet				
Firearm Type:	rifle - handgun - shotgun - airgun - black powder other:		Serial Number:	
Manufacturer:			Other Id No.:	
Caliber:			Capacity:	
Model/Type:			Weight:	
Barrel Length			Barrel Type:	Standard - Target - Bull - Other:
Finish:	Blue - Stainless - Parkerized - Plated (type): _____ other: _____			
Action: Circle all that apply	revolver - single shot - semiauto - full auto - lever - bolt - pump - top break - over/under - side by side - single action - double action - double action auto - muzzle loader			
Sight Type:			Stock Type:	
Scope Info:			Rings/Bases:	
Acquisition Information				
Obtained From:			Id No.:	
Name and address	^		DOB:	
^	^		Relationship:	
^	^		Date Purchased:	
Price Paid:	$		Replacement Value:	$
Special Or Specific Information				
Accessories:			Best Load:	
Special Marks Or Cartouches:			Maint Info:	
Other Notes:				
Disposition Information				
If I should die I want this firearm to go to:				
Gun Sold To:			Id No.:	
Name and address	^		DOB:	
^	^		Relationship:	
^	^		Date Sold:	
Selling Price:	$		Lost/Stolen:	

Additional Notes:

Photo:

Personal Firearms Basic Ownership Datasheet

Firearm Type:	rifle - handgun - shotgun - airgun - black powder other:	Serial Number:	
Manufacturer:		Other Id No.:	
Caliber:		Capacity:	
Model/Type:		Weight:	
Barrel Length		Barrel Type:	Standard - Target - Bull - Other:
Finish:	Blue - Stainless - Parkerized - Plated (type): _____ other: _____		
Action: Circle all that apply	revolver - single shot - semiauto - full auto - lever - bolt - pump - top break - over/under - side by side - single action - double action - double action auto - muzzle loader		
Sight Type:		Stock Type:	
Scope Info:		Rings/Bases:	

Acquisition Information

Obtained From:		Id No.:	
Name and address		DOB:	
		Relationship:	
		Date Purchased:	
Price Paid:	$	Replacement Value:	$

Special Or Specific Information

Accessories:		Best Load:	
Special Marks Or Cartouches:		Maint Info:	
Other Notes:			

Disposition Information

If I should die I want this firearm to go to:

Gun Sold To:		Id No.:	
Name and address		DOB:	
		Relationship:	
		Date Sold:	
Selling Price:	$	Lost/Stolen:	

Additional Notes:

Photo:

Personal Firearms Basic Ownership Datasheet

Firearm Type:	rifle - handgun - shotgun - airgun - black powder other:	Serial Number:	
Manufacturer:		Other Id No.:	
Caliber:		Capacity:	
Model/Type:		Weight:	
Barrel Length		Barrel Type:	Standard - Target - Bull - Other:
Finish:	Blue - Stainless - Parkerized - Plated (type): _____ other: _____		
Action: Circle all that apply	revolver - single shot - semiauto - full auto - lever - bolt - pump - top break - over/under - side by side - single action - double action - double action auto - muzzle loader		
Sight Type:		Stock Type:	
Scope Info:		Rings/Bases:	

Acquisition Information

Obtained From:		Id No.:	
Name and address		DOB:	
		Relationship:	
		Date Purchased:	
Price Paid:	$	Replacement Value:	$

Special Or Specific Information

Accessories:		Best Load:	
Special Marks Or Cartouches:		Maint Info:	
Other Notes:			

Disposition Information

If I should die I want this firearm to go to:

Gun Sold To:		Id No.:	
Name and address		DOB:	
		Relationship:	
		Date Sold:	
Selling Price:	$	Lost/Stolen:	

Additional Notes:

Photo:

Personal Firearms Basic Ownership Datasheet

Firearm Type:	rifle - handgun - shotgun - airgun - black powder other:	Serial Number:	
Manufacturer:		Other Id No.:	
Caliber:		Capacity:	
Model/Type:		Weight:	
Barrel Length		Barrel Type:	Standard - Target - Bull - Other:
Finish:	Blue - Stainless - Parkerized - Plated (type): _____ other: _____		
Action: Circle all that apply	revolver - single shot - semiauto - full auto - lever - bolt - pump - top break - over/under - side by side - single action - double action - double action auto - muzzle loader		
Sight Type:		Stock Type:	
Scope Info:		Rings/Bases:	

Acquisition Information

Obtained From:		Id No.:	
Name and address		DOB:	
		Relationship:	
		Date Purchased:	
Price Paid:	$	Replacement Value:	$

Special Or Specific Information

Accessories:		Best Load:	
Special Marks Or Cartouches:		Maint Info:	
Other Notes:			

Disposition Information

If I should die I want this firearm to go to:			
Gun Sold To:		Id No.:	
Name and address		DOB:	
		Relationship:	
		Date Sold:	
Selling Price:	$	Lost/Stolen:	

Additional Notes:

Photo:

Personal Firearms Basic Ownership Datasheet

Firearm Type:	rifle - handgun - shotgun - airgun - black powder other:	Serial Number:	
Manufacturer:		Other Id No.:	
Caliber:		Capacity:	
Model/Type:		Weight:	
Barrel Length		Barrel Type:	Standard - Target - Bull - Other:
Finish:	Blue - Stainless - Parkerized - Plated (type): _____ other: _____		
Action: Circle all that apply	revolver - single shot - semiauto - full auto - lever - bolt - pump - top break - over/under - side by side - single action - double action - double action auto - muzzle loader		
Sight Type:		Stock Type:	
Scope Info:		Rings/Bases:	

Acquisition Information

Obtained From:		Id No.:	
Name and address		DOB:	
		Relationship:	
		Date Purchased:	
Price Paid:	$	Replacement Value:	$

Special Or Specific Information

Accessories:		Best Load:	
Special Marks Or Cartouches:		Maint Info:	
Other Notes:			

Disposition Information

If I should die I want this firearm to go to:

Gun Sold To:		Id No.:	
Name and address		DOB:	
		Relationship:	
		Date Sold:	
Selling Price:	$	Lost/Stolen:	

Additional Notes:

Photo:

Personal Firearms Basic Ownership Datasheet

Firearm Type:	rifle - handgun - shotgun - airgun - black powder other:	**Serial Number:**	
Manufacturer:		**Other Id No.:**	
Caliber:		**Capacity:**	
Model/Type:		**Weight:**	
Barrel Length		**Barrel Type:**	Standard - Target - Bull - Other:
Finish:	Blue - Stainless - Parkerized - Plated (type): _____ other: _____		
Action: Circle all that apply	revolver - single shot - semiauto - full auto - lever - bolt - pump - top break - over/under - side by side - single action - double action - double action auto - muzzle loader		
Sight Type:		**Stock Type:**	
Scope Info:		**Rings/Bases:**	

Acquisition Information

Obtained From:		**Id No.:**	
Name and address		**DOB:**	
		Relationship:	
		Date Purchased:	
Price Paid:	$	**Replacement Value:**	$

Special Or Specific Information

Accessories:		**Best Load:**	
Special Marks Or Cartouches:		**Maint Info:**	
Other Notes:			

Disposition Information

If I should die I want this firearm to go to:			
Gun Sold To:		**Id No.:**	
Name and address		**DOB:**	
		Relationship:	
		Date Sold:	
Selling Price:	$	**Lost/Stolen:**	

Additional Notes:

Photo:

Personal Firearms Basic Ownership Datasheet

Firearm Type:	rifle - handgun - shotgun - airgun - black powder other:	**Serial Number:**	
Manufacturer:		**Other Id No.:**	
Caliber:		**Capacity:**	
Model/Type:		**Weight:**	
Barrel Length		**Barrel Type:**	Standard - Target - Bull - Other:
Finish:	Blue - Stainless - Parkerized - Plated (type): _____ other: _____		
Action: Circle all that apply	revolver - single shot - semiauto - full auto - lever - bolt - pump - top break - over/under - side by side - single action - double action - double action auto - muzzle loader		
Sight Type:		**Stock Type:**	
Scope Info:		**Rings/Bases:**	

Acquisition Information

Obtained From:		**Id No.:**	
Name and address		**DOB:**	
		Relationship:	
		Date Purchased:	
Price Paid:	$	**Replacement Value:**	$

Special Or Specific Information

Accessories:		**Best Load:**	
Special Marks Or Cartouches:		**Maint Info:**	
Other Notes:			

Disposition Information

If I should die I want this firearm to go to:

Gun Sold To:		**Id No.:**	
Name and address		**DOB:**	
		Relationship:	
		Date Sold:	
Selling Price:	$	**Lost/Stolen:**	

Additional Notes:

Photo:

Personal Firearms Basic Ownership Datasheet

Firearm Type:	rifle - handgun - shotgun - airgun - black powder other:	**Serial Number:**	
Manufacturer:		**Other Id No.:**	
Caliber:		**Capacity:**	
Model/Type:		**Weight:**	
Barrel Length		**Barrel Type:**	Standard - Target - Bull - Other:
Finish:	Blue - Stainless - Parkerized - Plated (type): _____ other: _____		
Action: Circle all that apply	revolver - single shot - semiauto - full auto - lever - bolt - pump - top break - over/under - side by side - single action - double action - double action auto - muzzle loader		
Sight Type:		**Stock Type:**	
Scope Info:		**Rings/Bases:**	

Acquisition Information

Obtained From:		**Id No.:**	
Name and address		**DOB:**	
		Relationship:	
		Date Purchased:	
Price Paid:	$	**Replacement Value:**	$

Special Or Specific Information

Accessories:		**Best Load:**	
Special Marks Or Cartouches:		**Maint Info:**	
Other Notes:			

Disposition Information

If I should die I want this firearm to go to:

Gun Sold To:		**Id No.:**	
Name and address		**DOB:**	
		Relationship:	
		Date Sold:	
Selling Price:	$	**Lost/Stolen:**	

Additional Notes:

Photo:

Personal Firearms Basic Ownership Datasheet

Firearm Type:	rifle - handgun - shotgun - airgun - black powder other:	Serial Number:	
Manufacturer:		Other Id No.:	
Caliber:		Capacity:	
Model/Type:		Weight:	
Barrel Length		Barrel Type:	Standard - Target - Bull - Other:
Finish:	Blue - Stainless - Parkerized - Plated (type): _____ other: _____		
Action: Circle all that apply	revolver - single shot - semiauto - full auto - lever - bolt - pump - top break - over/under - side by side - single action - double action - double action auto - muzzle loader		
Sight Type:		Stock Type:	
Scope Info:		Rings/Bases:	

Acquisition Information

Obtained From:		Id No.:	
Name and address		DOB:	
		Relationship:	
		Date Purchased:	
Price Paid:	$	Replacement Value:	$

Special Or Specific Information

Accessories:		Best Load:	
Special Marks Or Cartouches:		Maint Info:	
Other Notes:			

Disposition Information

If I should die I want this firearm to go to:

Gun Sold To:		Id No.:	
Name and address		DOB:	
		Relationship:	
		Date Sold:	
Selling Price:	$	Lost/Stolen:	

Additional Notes:

Photo:

Personal Firearms Basic Ownership Datasheet

Firearm Type:	rifle - handgun - shotgun - airgun - black powder other:	**Serial Number:**	
Manufacturer:		**Other Id No.:**	
Caliber:		**Capacity:**	
Model/Type:		**Weight:**	
Barrel Length		**Barrel Type:**	Standard - Target - Bull - Other:
Finish:	Blue - Stainless - Parkerized - Plated (type): _____ other: _____		
Action: Circle all that apply	revolver - single shot - semiauto - full auto - lever - bolt - pump - top break - over/under - side by side - single action - double action - double action auto - muzzle loader		
Sight Type:		**Stock Type:**	
Scope Info:		**Rings/Bases:**	

Acquisition Information

Obtained From:		**Id No.:**	
Name and address		**DOB:**	
		Relationship:	
		Date Purchased:	
Price Paid:	$	**Replacement Value:**	$

Special Or Specific Information

Accessories:		**Best Load:**	
Special Marks Or Cartouches:		**Maint Info:**	
Other Notes:			

Disposition Information

If I should die I want this firearm to go to:

Gun Sold To:		**Id No.:**	
Name and address		**DOB:**	
		Relationship:	
		Date Sold:	
Selling Price:	$	**Lost/Stolen:**	

Additional Notes:

Photo:

Personal Firearms Basic Ownership Datasheet

Firearm Type:	rifle - handgun - shotgun - airgun - black powder other:	**Serial Number:**	
Manufacturer:		**Other Id No.:**	
Caliber:		**Capacity:**	
Model/Type:		**Weight:**	
Barrel Length		**Barrel Type:**	Standard - Target - Bull - Other:
Finish:	Blue - Stainless - Parkerized - Plated (type): _____ other: _____		
Action: Circle all that apply	revolver - single shot - semiauto - full auto - lever - bolt - pump - top break - over/under - side by side - single action - double action - double action auto - muzzle loader		
Sight Type:		**Stock Type:**	
Scope Info:		**Rings/Bases:**	

Acquisition Information

Obtained From:		**Id No.:**	
Name and address		**DOB:**	
		Relationship:	
		Date Purchased:	
Price Paid:	$	**Replacement Value:**	$

Special Or Specific Information

Accessories:		**Best Load:**	
Special Marks Or Cartouches:		**Maint Info:**	
Other Notes:			

Disposition Information

If I should die I want this firearm to go to:			
Gun Sold To:		**Id No.:**	
Name and address		**DOB:**	
		Relationship:	
		Date Sold:	
Selling Price:	$	**Lost/Stolen:**	

Additional Notes:

Photo:

Personal Firearms Basic Ownership Datasheet

Firearm Type:	rifle - handgun - shotgun - airgun - black powder other:	**Serial Number:**	
Manufacturer:		**Other Id No.:**	
Caliber:		**Capacity:**	
Model/Type:		**Weight:**	
Barrel Length		**Barrel Type:**	Standard - Target - Bull - Other:
Finish:	Blue - Stainless - Parkerized - Plated (type): _____ other: _____		
Action: Circle all that apply	revolver - single shot - semiauto - full auto - lever - bolt - pump - top break - over/under - side by side - single action - double action - double action auto - muzzle loader		
Sight Type:		**Stock Type:**	
Scope Info:		**Rings/Bases:**	

Acquisition Information

Obtained From:		**Id No.:**	
Name and address		**DOB:**	
		Relationship:	
		Date Purchased:	
Price Paid:	$	**Replacement Value:**	$

Special Or Specific Information

Accessories:		**Best Load:**	
Special Marks Or Cartouches:		**Maint Info:**	
Other Notes:			

Disposition Information

If I should die I want this firearm to go to:

Gun Sold To:		**Id No.:**	
Name and address		**DOB:**	
		Relationship:	
		Date Sold:	
Selling Price:	$	**Lost/Stolen:**	

Additional Notes:

Photo:

Personal Firearms Basic Ownership Datasheet

Firearm Type:	rifle - handgun - shotgun - airgun - black powder other:	Serial Number:	
Manufacturer:		Other Id No.:	
Caliber:		Capacity:	
Model/Type:		Weight:	
Barrel Length		Barrel Type:	Standard - Target - Bull - Other:
Finish:	Blue - Stainless - Parkerized - Plated (type): _____ other: _____		
Action: Circle all that apply	revolver - single shot - semiauto - full auto - lever - bolt - pump - top break - over/under - side by side - single action - double action - double action auto - muzzle loader		
Sight Type:		Stock Type:	
Scope Info:		Rings/Bases:	

Acquisition Information

Obtained From:		Id No.:	
Name and address		DOB:	
		Relationship:	
		Date Purchased:	
Price Paid:	$	Replacement Value:	$

Special Or Specific Information

Accessories:		Best Load:	
Special Marks Or Cartouches:		Maint Info:	
Other Notes:			

Disposition Information

If I should die I want this firearm to go to:			
Gun Sold To:		Id No.:	
Name and address		DOB:	
		Relationship:	
		Date Sold:	
Selling Price:	$	Lost/Stolen:	

Additional Notes:

Photo:

Personal Firearms Record Book

Personalized Index Pages:

Use these pages to keep track of which page each gun is on. This should make it easier to flip straight to the page you are looking for without the need for intensive search.

GUN	**Page Number**
	1
	3
	5
	7
	9
	11
	13
	15
	17
	19
	21
	23
	25
	27
	29
	31
	33
	35
	37
	39
	41
	43
	45
	47
	49
	51
	53
	55
	57
	59
	61
	63
	65
	67
	69
	71
	73

	75
	77
	79
	81
	83
	85
	87
	89
	91
	93
	95
	97
	99
	101
	103
	105
	107
	109
	111
	113
	115
	117
	119
	121
	123
	125
	127
	129
	131
	133
	135
	137
	139
	141
	143
	145
	147
	149
Personalized Index pages	151
About the Author	153

ABOUT THE AUTHOR

The Author/Creator of this Firearms Record Book is an avid Gun Owner, collector, shooter and hunter. It is a strong belief that keeping track of your OWN guns is far safer and more effective than letting the Government know your every detail.

Made in the USA
San Bernardino, CA
24 December 2013